FA
S
CUTIES

Pretty Birds

Books published by Running Press are available at special discounts for bulk
purchases in the United States by corporations, institutions, and other
organizations. For more information, please contact the Special Markets
Department at the Perseus Books Group, 2300 Chestnut Street, Suite 200,
Philadelphia, PA 19103, or call (800) 810-4145, ext. 5000, or e-mail special.
markets@perseusbooks.com.

ISBN: 978-0-7624-5385-6
Library of Congress Control Number: 2014942369

Ebook ISBN: 978-0-7624-5644-4

9   8   7   6   5   4   3   2   1
Digit on the right indicates the number of this printing

Art Director: Lucy Smith
Cover Design: Lucy Smith & Michelle Rowlandson
Book layout: Michelle Rowlandson
Illustrations: Jess Hibbert
Photography: Ivan Jones
Commissioning Editor: Jacqueline Ford
Project Editor: Cath Senker
Assistant Editor: Tamsin Richardson

Running Press Book Publishers
2300 Chestnut Street
Philadelphia, PA 19103-4371

Visit us on the web!
www.runningpress.com

FABRIC
STASH
CUTIES

Pretty Birds

18 simple projects to sew and love

VIRGINIA LINDSAY

Running Press
PHILADELPHIA · LONDON

Contents

Introduction

I have so many fabric scraps that if I dumped them onto the floor of my sewing room, the heap would be as big as a fall-leaf pile! Although I try to be as economical as possible when using my fabrics, there always seems to be some waste and odd shapes that are left over after a project is complete. If you have been sewing as much and as long as me, that creates A LOT of pieces! Making these birds was such a fun and useful way to sew with some of those pieces. I loved searching through my fabric stash to find the right colors, textures, and prints for each bird.

The projects in this book range from quick and easy (the white Dove) to moderately challenging (the Hummingbird) but all are created to be fun and satisfying. From cute (the Canary) and trendy (the Owl) to classic (the Woodpecker) and elegant (the Swan), the 18 projects in this book should satisfy every crafty mood you are feeling. If you are an avid bird lover or simply someone looking to make some sweet sewing projects, this is the sewing book for you.

Each project has pattern templates to download and print—please see pages 8–9 for how to do this. Follow the guidelines on your pattern pieces closely. Working with small pieces of fabric can be frustrating at first, so be patient and go slowly the first time you make one of the birds. Basting (handsewing a loose running stitch) instead of pinning before you machine sew can work wonders when working on small pieces.

Although I do the majority of the sewing on these projects with my sewing machine, the patterns are also suitable for handsewing if you prefer. All the birds do require a certain amount of handsewing anyway, and it's an important part of the process to get your birds looking authentic.

Since creating these birds is essentially doll making, there are also some special materials that you will need to have on hand along with your scrap fabrics. Wool felt (not too thick but high quality) makes lovely and long-lasting beaks, feet, and crests on your birds. Synthetic felt is a very inferior substitute. You will also need a variety of coordinating separated embroidery floss and needle floss, and embroidery-floss needles to match the felt and the fabric.

As well as the main project, you will also find suggested practical uses for each of the birds. Be sure to take advantage of these ideas and to transform these birds into your own creative household items too. I truly hope you enjoy sewing these birds as much as I enjoyed created them. Your scraps bin is calling your name to begin sewing up these very special fabric stash cuties!

Virginia Lindsay

Virginia Lindsay

How to use this book

Sewing

When you sew seams, note that seam allowances are $\frac{1}{4}$ in. (6 mm), and use straight stitch (or running stitch if handsewing) unless specified otherwise. All seam allowances have been included within the patterns. Handsewing stitches should be $\frac{1}{16}$–$\frac{1}{8}$ in. (2–3 mm) long and evenly spaced. The thinner the fabric, the smaller the stitches. Always backstitch at the beginning and end of every seam and clip the threads. Separate embroidery floss, into three strands for sewing.

Downloading the pattern templates

Scan the QR code (A) at the top of the page with your smartphone or webcam attached to your computer. Note that you will need to have a QR code reader installed on your device. These readers are usually free to download.

Alternatively, type in the address printed under the QR code (B) in your web browser.

If you are copying the template direct from the book the scale of the pattern on the page has been included (C) so you know how much to scale it up by when you copy it.

On the web page, you will see a button to download the pattern (D).

Printing the pattern templates

The pattern templates are designed to be printed at 100%. Before printing the patterns, make sure that page scaling is set to None in the Adobe Acrobat print window.

The pattern pieces are all made to fit together perfectly but do not be afraid to make your own adjustments. For example, it is very simple to enlarge your birds by copying the pattern pieces and printing them out on your home printer at 150 or even 200%. Also, you may want to lengthen tail feathers, increase wing sizes, head size, and even belly size. Just be aware that increasing the size of one piece may affect the way it fits with another piece.

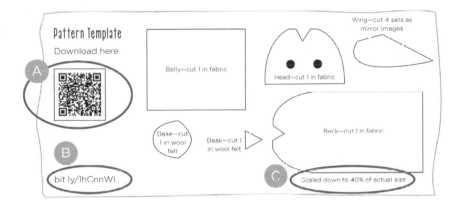

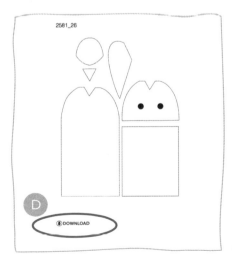

Projects

Owl

Owls have long represented wisdom and scholarship. There is something about their unique shape and big round eyes that is just so appealing. Just one warning note—making fabric owls is addictive. I have been doing it for years and I still love it.

These fun little friends are a quick and easy sew, and you can use a variety of fabric combinations. Feel free to use bright and funky colors; the Owl's shape and features are so distinctive that it's always obvious what you are making. You can search for all your favorite fabric scraps and use them up for this project. The Owl pattern can be used to make toys, door stops, cable caddies, and fun pillows. Be sure to use good-quality wool felt so the eyes and base do not become spoiled after a few big owl hugs!

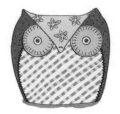

Get stitching!

Materials needed

- Cotton fabric scraps in 3 colors
- Wool felt in 2 colors, 1 for eyes and 1 coordinating with cotton fabrics for base
- Sewing machine (optional), thread, scissors
- Polyester fiberfill
- Needle and thread
- Separated coordinating embroidery floss
- 2½-in. (1.3-cm) buttons

Pattern measures

Height: 5½ in. (14 cm)
Width: 5 in. (13 cm)

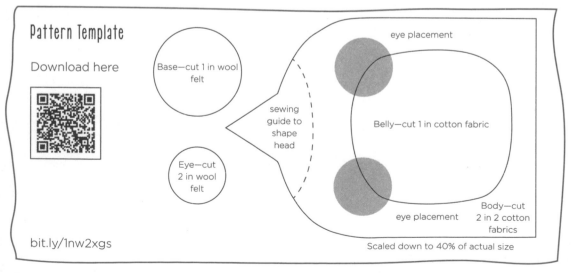

Pattern Template

Download here

bit.ly/1nw2xgs

Base—cut 1 in wool felt

Eye—cut 2 in wool felt

sewing guide to shape head

eye placement

Belly—cut 1 in cotton fabric

eye placement

Body—cut 2 in 2 cotton fabrics

Scaled down to 40% of actual size

Step 1

Cut out all the pattern pieces according to the guidelines.

Step 2

Zigzag stitch the belly piece onto the front body. Switch back to straight stitch and sew on the felt eyes. To handsew, use blanket or overcast stitch then running stitch. The pattern piece has a placement guide to help you.

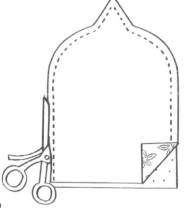

Step 3

Pin the front and back pieces right sides together. Leave the base open but sew up the side to the point and then back down the other side. Trim the seams down and then clip the fabric at the tip.

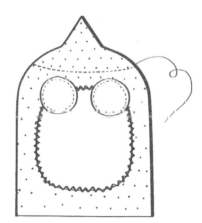

Step 4

Turn right side out and press flat. The pattern piece has a guide for sewing the ears. Do this with the sewing machine by marking with pins where you want to begin and end and then just sew a curve above the eyes.

Step 5

Stuff the Owl with polyester fiberfill. Knot
the end of a piece of thread and then sew a
running stitch around the base of the Owl.
Gently pull the thread to gather the fabric
together. Secure the gathered fabric with a
strong knot.

Step 6

Handsew on the base felt piece to cover
up the gathered fabric. Use matching
embroidery floss and a simple running
stitch to secure the felt onto the base.

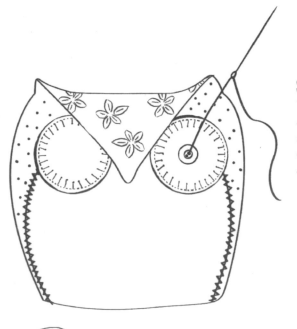

Step 7

To finish, sew the button eyes in place
and sew the beak down with a couple of
stitches. You can really make the eyes stand
out by doing a simple decorative stitch
around the circumference of the eyes.

Other ideas to try

Small hot-water bottle cover

Because of its shape the Owl is perfect to transform into a small hot-water bottle cover for chilly nights. Consider using heat-insulated batting to give your hot water bottle longer-lasting warmth. You could use flannel and minky fabric for the exterior pieces to create an extra cozy bottle cover. Turn to page 121 for additional templates, QR codes, and full instructions.

Headphone or cable caddy

Add a simple pocket to the back of the Owl. Use a scrap of fabric 6¼ x 9 in. (16 x 23 cm) to make a piece that is 6¼ x 4½ in. (16 x 11.5 cm). Fold the fabric in half lengthwise, wrong sides together, to make a pocket. Line it up with the base of the back piece and tack it to the sides. In Step 3, sew through the pocket layer when you sew the front and back sides together. Finish the Owl as usual but now you will have a nice little pocket in the back. Keep it on your desk next to your computer!

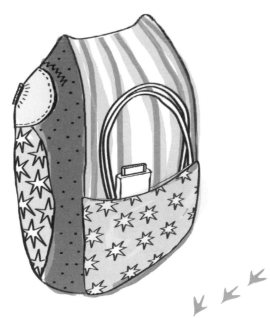

Canary

This bright yellow Canary will make a delightful sewing project, and what better color to use than canary yellow to make it? Of course, you can use any color you have on hand though.

You might like to consider using a solid yellow for the main body and save your fun prints for the belly, tail, and wings. A fine whale corduroy or fuzzy flannel would also make a fun addition to the Canary's body. It is important to stuff the body nice and full to achieve the proper round shape of this bird. When you think you have filled it, add a little more stuffing!

Get stitching!

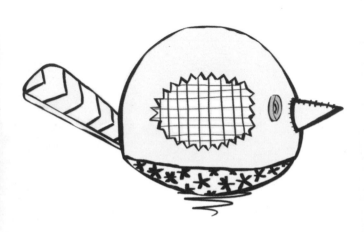

Materials needed

- Fabric scraps in shades of of 1 color
- Sewing machine (optional), coordinating thread, scissors
- Scrap of fusible interfacing
- Chopstick for turning
- Polyester fiberfill
- Pinking shears
- Scrap of wool felt
- Separated coordinating embroidery floss and needle
- 2 buttons

Pattern measures

Height: 2¾ in. (7 cm)
Length: 5½ in. (14 cm)

Pattern Template

Download here

bit.ly/1noCNoR

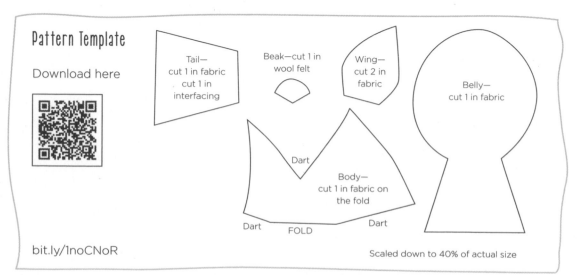

Tail—cut 1 in fabric cut 1 in interfacing

Beak—cut 1 in wool felt

Wing—cut 2 in fabric

Belly—cut 1 in fabric

Dart

Body—cut 1 in fabric on the fold

Dart

Dart   FOLD   Dart

Scaled down to 40% of actual size

 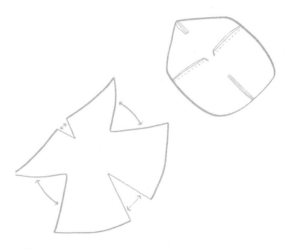

Step 1

Gather materials and cut out pattern pieces. Make sure you cut the body piece on the fold to give a double shape.

Step 2

Sew all four darts on the body pattern piece. Trim the seams of each dart.

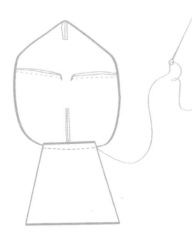 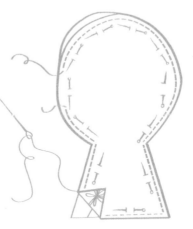

Step 3

Fuse the interfacing to the tail piece and then sew the tail to the body piece, right sides together.

Step 4

Pin and sew the belly onto the body/tail piece. Leave a 2-in. (5-cm) opening on the side for turning.

Step 5

Turn right side out, poke out the corners of the tail with a chopstick, and press the tail flat. Topstitch over the seam between the tail and the body piece.

Step 6

Stuff the body nice and full. Close the opening with a ladder stitch.

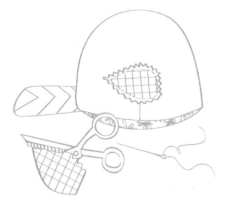

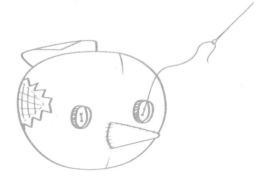

Step 7

Use pinking shears around the perimeter of the wing pieces. Handsew the wings onto the body with a running stitch, placing them so that they cover the darts.

Step 8

Fold the beak piece together. Use divided coordinating embroidery floss to sew the beak with a ladder stitch along the straight edge. Attach the beak to the face with the remaining floss. Sew button eyes onto the body on either side of the beak.

Other ideas to try

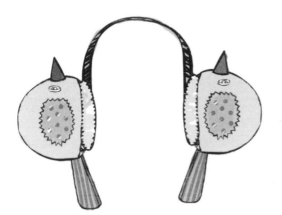

Ear muffs

Make two canaries and handsew a 3-in. (7.5-cm) circle of soft material, such as chenille or minky, to the bellies of the birds. Leave an opening on the top of the circles so that you can slide a 1 in. (2.5 cm)-wide plastic headband into each circle and secure it to the birds. If you want to attach it more firmly, you can add some glue to the bottom of the headband before you insert it into the soft fabric pieces.

Kitten toy

Kitties love bird toys, and the shape of this one is perfect for a kitty to play with. Embroider the eyes instead of using buttons and attach a long piece of string to the top of the head. Alternatively, stuff the bird with a rattle or something else your kitty will love!

Penguin

Penguins make everyone smile with their funny walk and rounded shape. There is just something happy and cute about penguins. Making fabric penguins is fun and simple. You could try making different sizes and create a whole family. These little guys will fill up your sewing room before you know it.

It's easy to get creative with this little project. Consider fabric and color when making your Penguin. My version has a terry-cloth belly for added texture. Since the shape of a Penguin is easily recognizable, you can use a variety of colors and prints and it'll still be obvious it's a Penguin. How about pink polka-dot fabric? No problem! Instead of making a flat beak, you can easily shape the beak into a cone and make it more realistic.

Get stitching!

Materials needed

- Fabric scraps in 2 colors
- Sewing machine (optional), thread, scissors
- Polyester fiberfill
- Needle and thread
- Wool felt
- Separated embroidery floss coordinating with felt
- 2 x ½-in. (1.3-cm) buttons

Pattern measures

Height: 5½ in. (14 cm)
Width: 2¾ in. (7 cm)

Pattern Template

Download here

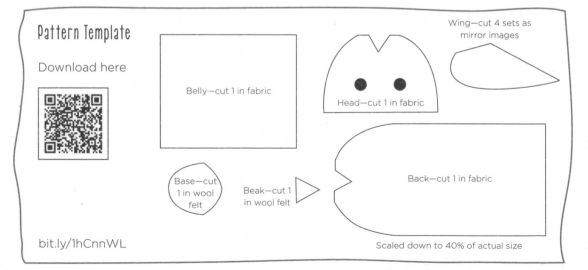

Belly—cut 1 in fabric

Wing—cut 4 sets as mirror images

Head—cut 1 in fabric

Base—cut 1 in wool felt

Beak—cut 1 in wool felt

Back—cut 1 in fabric

bit.ly/1hCnnWL

Scaled down to 40% of actual size

Step 1

Cut out all the pattern pieces according to the guidelines. Make sure that you cut out the wing sets as mirror images.

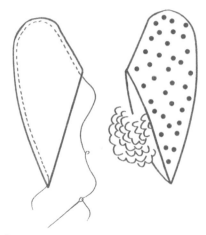

Step 2

To construct the wings, take two wing pieces and sew right sides together along the curved edge. Leave the straight edge open. Trim down the seams and turn right side out. Push a small amount of polyester fiberfill inside the wing and sew it closed. Repeat with the other wing pieces.

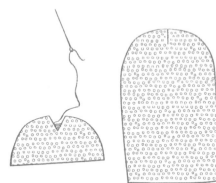

Step 3

Sew the dart on the head piece by folding the right sides together and sewing them closed. Sew the dart on the back piece the same way.

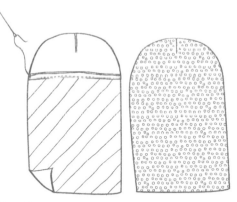

Step 4

Sew the head to the belly piece, right sides together. The head/belly will match up with the back piece.

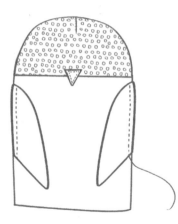 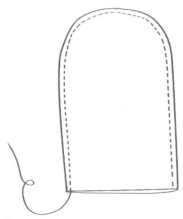

Step 5

Attach the wings to the belly. Pin the wings, pointing in toward the center of the belly piece and a little below the head and belly seam. Sew in place. Also, sew on the felt beak, centered, over the belly and head seam.

Step 6

Pin the back and front right sides together. Leave the base open and sew up the side, around the curved top, and down the other side. Make sure the wings stay in place between the layers. Trim the seams.

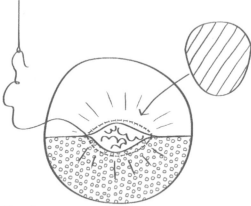 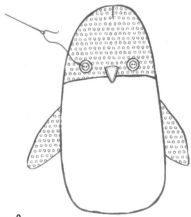

Step 7

Turn the piece right side out and stuff. Sew running stitch around the base, about 1/4 in. (6 mm) from the edges. Pull the thread gently to gather the fabric and knot it. With embroidery thread, sew the wool felt over the bottom so it can be seen from the front.

Step 8

Sew the button eyes on either side of the beak.

Other ideas to try

Puppet

Cut out two additional pieces the same size as the back piece. Instead of stuffing the Penguin as in Step 7, make the extra back pieces into a lining for the Penguin by sewing the lining and Penguin right sides together at the base. Leave a space for turning it right side out. Close up the opening and press flat. A child's hand will fit perfectly inside!

Pin cushion

Before Step 7, use a funnel to add some rice or popcorn kernels to weight the base of the Penguin. Then sew on the felt base and the button eyes. Stick in some new pins and needles and you have a darling gift for a sewing friend.

Dove

Doves bring so many sweet thoughts to mind—love, peace, kindness, serenity, marriage, and innocence. Their pretty shape and lovely wings make them a perfect sewing project. You can use doves as gift tags, pillow decorations, or ornaments. Once you've mastered the technique, try making several at once so that you always have something pretty and handmade to offer at special occasions such as weddings, baptisms, first communions, or birthdays.

This project is very quick and easy to make because the Dove is flat and requires no stuffing, so it's ideal as a beginner project. For your Dove, choose a soft, bright cotton and search for a piece of pretty lace for the wing decoration. You could also add rick rack to the wing for a more casual look or satin ribbon to dress up the Dove a little.

Get stitching!

Materials needed

- Cotton fabric scraps in 1 color
- Cotton batting
- Separated dark gray embroidery floss and needle
- Sewing machine (optional), thread, scissors
- Pinking shears
- Lace scrap
- Scrap of wool felt
- Separated embroidery floss to coordinate with wool felt

Pattern measures

Height: 4³/₄ in. (12 cm)
Length: 7 in. (18 cm)

Pattern Template

Download here

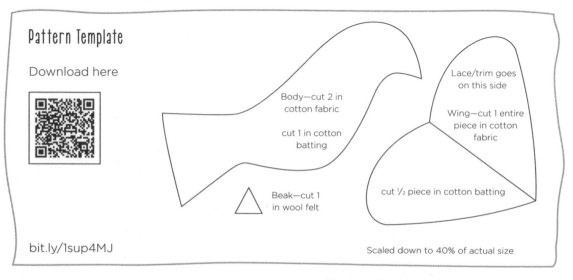

Body—cut 2 in cotton fabric

cut 1 in cotton batting

Lace/trim goes on this side

Wing—cut 1 entire piece in cotton fabric

Beak—cut 1 in wool felt

cut ½ piece in cotton batting

bit.ly/1sup4MJ

Scaled down to 40% of actual size

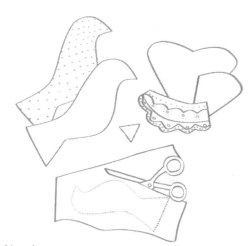

Step 1
Cut out all the pattern pieces according to the guidelines.

Step 2
Layer the cotton batting behind one piece of the body material. Embroider a closed eyelid with the gray floss and needle.

Step 3
Layer the other body piece on the other side of the cotton batting and pin the fabrics together. Sew around the entire perimeter of the Dove body. Trim down the seam with pinking shears.

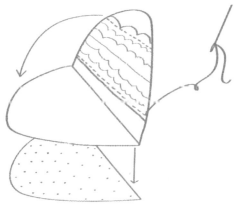

Step 4
Sew lace to the right side of the wing piece. Fold the wing right sides together and layer the cotton batting piece beneath the folded wing.

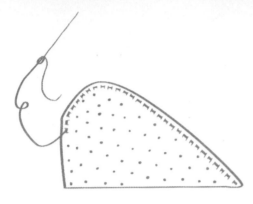

Step 5

Pin together and sew around the sides but leave a 1½-in. (4-cm) opening for turning. Next, turn the wing right side out and press it flat. Tuck the raw edges of the wing opening in to match the seam and press again.

Step 6

Topstitch around the perimeter of the wing. Pin the wing to the Dove body and, following the topstitching, sew the wing onto the body.

Step 7

Use the embroidery floss to sew the beak onto the Dove body with a split stitch.

Other ideas to try

Gift topper

Once you have made the Dove, either handsew on a thin ribbon or rick rack, or add the ribbon in Step 3 as you are sewing around the body of the Dove. Tie it around a gift as an elegant, handmade finishing touch.

Ring-bearer pillow

For a casual handmade wedding, the Dove can be sewn onto a lacy pillow to make a sweet ring-bearer pillow. The wing can serve as a perfect small pocket for a ring!

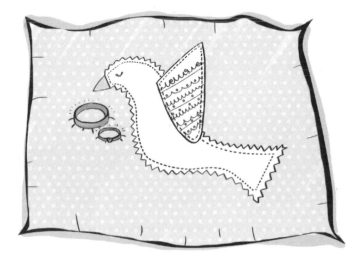

Eagle

Everyone knows that eagles are powerful and mysterious but I bet you didn't know they also look really cute made out of fabric! Eagles made from your scraps are fun and simple and as soon as you make one, you will have all the eagle lovers singing your praises.

Search through your scraps to find black and white fabric to make a simple Bald Eagle or search for golden browns to make a pretty Golden Eagle. You could easily increase the size of the pattern pieces and make a pillow for your child to cuddle. Make sure to pay special attention to the beak on this project. Before you start, you may want to experiment with a few well-placed stitches to get the special look of a hooked beak on your little omnivore.

Get stitching!

Materials needed

- Scraps of fabric in 1 light and 1 dark color
- Scrap of cotton batting
- Pinking shears
- Polyester fiberfill
- Sewing machine (optional), thread, scissors
- Wool felt
- Needle and thread
- Separated embroidery floss coordinating with wool felt
- Black buttons ½ in. (1.3 cm) or smaller

Pattern measures

Height: 8 in. (20 cm)
Width: 9½ in. (24 cm)

Pattern Template

Download here

bit.ly/1fUlutk

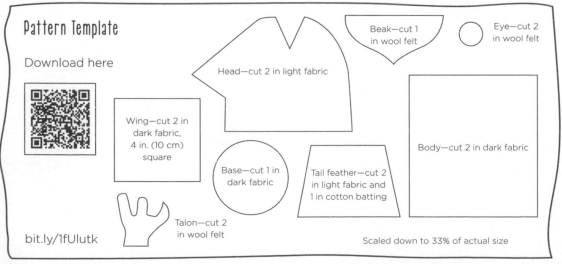

Head—cut 2 in light fabric

Beak—cut 1 in wool felt

Eye—cut 2 in wool felt

Wing—cut 2 in dark fabric, 4 in. (10 cm) square

Base—cut 1 in dark fabric

Tail feather—cut 2 in light fabric and 1 in cotton batting

Body—cut 2 in dark fabric

Talon—cut 2 in wool felt

Scaled down to 33% of actual size

Step 1

Cut out all the pattern pieces according to the guidelines. If you use a print for the head piece, make sure that you cut out the two pieces as mirror images.

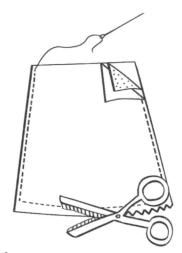

Step 2

To make the tail feathers, layer together a cotton piece, cotton batting, and then another cotton piece. Right sides are facing out. Topstitch around the three sides and finish the raw edges with the pinking shears.

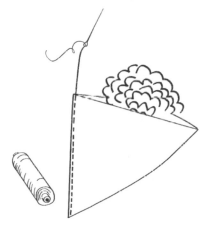

Step 3

Fold the right sides of a wing piece together to make a triangle. Sew together one of the edges. Turn right side out. Put a little bit of stuffing into the wing piece. Close up the wing by topstitching the open edges closed. Repeat with the other wing piece.

Step 4

Trim the bottom of the head pieces with pinking shears. Place the head pieces so that the bottom edge of the head overlaps the top edge of the body piece. The heads should be mirror images. Pin and zigzag stitch the head pieces onto the body pieces. Use overcast stitch if handsewing.

Step 5

Attach the wings to the body by basting them on facing in toward the center of the front side. Baste the talons onto the front body at the base, pointing in toward the center also. Baste the tail piece onto the bottom edge of the back body piece.

Step 6

On both head pieces, fold the right sides of the darts together and sew closed. Layer the back and front body pieces right sides together and pin. Sew up the sides and around the head but leave the base open. Trim the seams down.

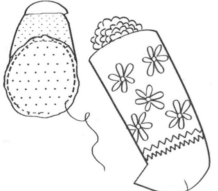

Step 7

Pin the base piece onto the body piece with right sides facing. Sew the pieces together but leave an opening of 1½ in. (4cm) where the tail and the base meet. Trim the seams, turn the piece right side out, and stuff with polyester fiberfill. Sew the opening closed by hand.

Step 8

Fold the felt beak to match the curved edges and, using coordinating embroidery floss, sew closed with a ladder stitch. Place the beak over the pointed beak area on the head and stitch in place. Layer the eye circles beneath the black buttons and sew on button eyes.

Other ideas to try

Doorstop

The Eagle's shape make it perfect for a cute doorstop. Enlarge the pattern to 125%. In Step 5, fill the bottom half with something heavy, such as rice, popcorn kernels, or beans, and stuff the top half with polyester fiberfill.

Remote control holder

Attach a piece of 1 x 4¼ in. (2.5 x 11 cm) elastic to the back of the Eagle between the wings. You can handsew the elastic on or tack it to the back body during Step 5. Very cute!

Kookaburra

The laughing call of the kookaburra has made it a famous bird across the world but this funny guy is actually native to Australia. The kookaburra is distinctive for its big beak, mask, and long tail feathers and was one of the mascots for the 2000 Summer Olympics in Sydney. There is even a children's song all about the bird's distinctive laughter.

The main shape of this bird is quick to make. The mask is simply sewn on with the raw edges exposed so the fraying gives a little texture to the rounded head. The beak can be made using two shades of brown felt for a realistic look but you can substitute another color if necessary. The Kookaburra's wing is attached like a cape to give it a sturdy, regal look.

Get stitching!

Materials needed

- Scraps of cotton fabric in shades of the same color
- Sewing machine (optional), coordinating thread, scissors
- Polyester fiberfill
- Needle and thread
- 2 shades of the same color wool felt for the beak
- Wool felt for base
- Separated embroidery floss to coordinate with the beak
- 2 x ½-in. (1.3-cm) buttons

Pattern measures

Height: 9½ in. (24 cm)
Width: 3 in. (8 cm)

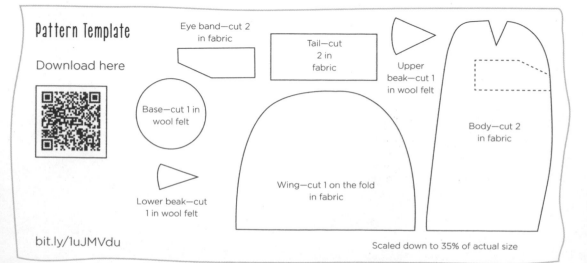

Pattern Template

Download here

bit.ly/1uJMVdu

Eye band—cut 2 in fabric

Tail—cut 2 in fabric

Upper beak—cut 1 in wool felt

Base—cut 1 in wool felt

Lower beak—cut 1 in wool felt

Wing—cut 1 on the fold in fabric

Body—cut 2 in fabric

Scaled down to 35% of actual size

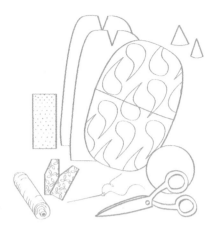

Step 1

Cut out all the pattern pieces according to the guidelines.

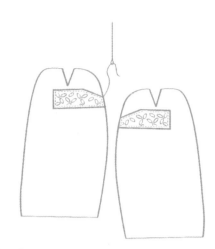

Step 2

Lay an eye band, right side facing up, on each body piece. Pin them in place. Sew on the eye bands with an overcast stitch as close to the edge as possible. The raw edges are left exposed and will fray a little to add texture.

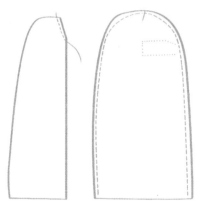

Step 3

Create the darts on the body pieces by folding the right sides of the small triangle at the top of the head together and sewing closed. Pin and sew the right sides of the bodies together. Leave the base open.

Step 4

Trim seams and turn the body right side out. Stuff it with fiberfill. Tie a knot at the end of a piece of thread. Sew a running stitch around the base about 1/4 in. (6 mm) from the raw edge. Gently pull the thread to gather the base together. Knot to secure.

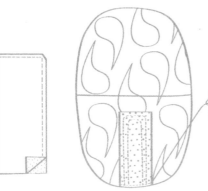

Step 5

Sew three sides of the tail pieces right sides together, leaving a short end open for turning. Trim seams and turn right side out. Press flat and topstitch the tail for decorative effect. Center the tail on the curved edge of the wing piece, pointed in toward the center. Baste in place.

Step 6

Fold the wing piece right sides together and pin in place. Sew around the curve, leaving a 2-in. (5-cm) opening for turning. Trim seams and turn right side out. Press flat and topstitch around the perimeter to close the opening. Handsew the flat top edge onto the body.

Step 7

Using separated embroidery floss, sew together the two sides of the beak with a ladder stitch. The larger side will curve up when sewn to the bottom. Sew the beak onto the body where the eye bands meet. Sew on the button eyes.

Step 8

With embroidery floss, use a ladder stitch or blanket stitch to attach the base to the bottom of the body and cover up the gathered fabric you made in Step 4.

Other ideas to try

Pencil holder

The Kookaburra sits nicely on the edge of your desk or bookshelf if the bottom is weighted by some rice or beans during the stuffing in Step 4. Use a piece of wool felt to make a small pocket that measures 2 x 3 in. (5 x 7.5 cm). In Step 6, after the wing is topstitched but before you sew it to the body, center the pocket about 1 in. (2.5 cm) above the tail. Pin and sew the three sides to secure the pocket. Attach the wing as instructed in Step 6.

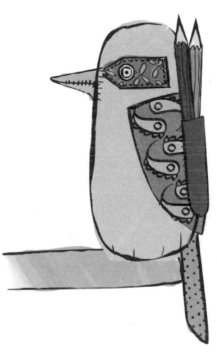

Car air freshener

In Step 4, stuff the Kookaburra's head with polyester fiberfill and stuff the center with strong-smelling potpourri. Finish stuffing with fiberfill and close up the body as directed. When you have finished making the Kookaburra, handsew a piece of 8-in. (20-cm) elastic cording onto the top of the head.

Bluebird

Catching a glimpse of a beautiful bluebird on the edge of the woods is a sure sign that spring is in full swing. Bluebirds are big helpers in the garden since they eat pest insects, and they are a symbol of happiness and cheer in many songs and poems. Their simple shape and pretty colors make bluebirds a great little sewing project!

Quilting cottons of similar weight are the best choice to make this little bird. The wing could be replaced with a lightweight corduroy or denim to give extra texture and interest if you choose. Using sturdy wool felt for the beak will insure a nice shape and is worth the extra effort. Most of this project is done on a sewing machine (you can sew by hand if preferred) although a little handsewing is required for making the gathered belly and embroidering the eye.

Get stitching!

Materials needed

- 4 scraps of fabric, 2 shades in each of 2 colors
- Sewing machine (optional), coordinating thread, scissors
- Needle and thread
- Small piece of dark wool felt
- Separated embroidery floss to coordinate with wool felt
- Polyester fiberfill

Pattern measures

Length: 6¼ in. (16 cm)
Width: 2 in. (5 cm)

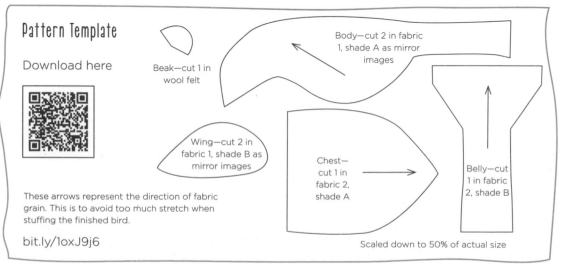

Pattern Template

Download here

Beak—cut 1 in wool felt

Body—cut 2 in fabric 1, shade A as mirror images

Wing—cut 2 in fabric 1, shade B as mirror images

Chest—cut 1 in fabric 2, shade A

Belly—cut 1 in fabric 2, shade B

These arrows represent the direction of fabric grain. This is to avoid too much stretch when stuffing the finished bird.

bit.ly/1oxJ9j6

Scaled down to 50% of actual size

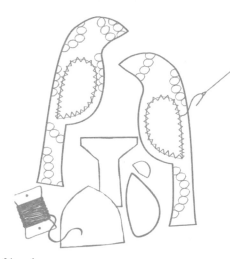

Step 1

Trace the pattern pieces onto your fabric. Follow the pattern piece guidelines and cut them out. With right sides facing up, position the wings on the body pieces using the body pattern pieces to guide you, and zigzag stitch the wings in place. Use overcast stitch if handsewing.

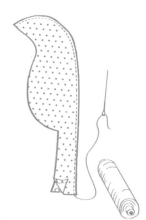

Step 2

Place the two body pieces together, right sides facing. Using coordinating thread, sew the top curved edge together with a ¼ in. (6 mm), or less, seam allowance. Do not sew all the way to the pointed tip, but instead stop ¼ in. (6 mm) short, and backstitch. Finger press the seam open.

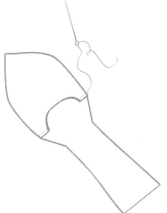

Step 3

Take the chest and belly pieces and lay them together, right sides facing. You will see that the chest is wider than the belly. Sew together only the sides, about ½ in. (1.3 cm), and leave the gap in the middle open. Finger press open the seam.

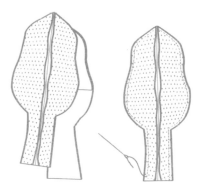

Step 4

Open up the body pieces. Starting at the pointed tip, evenly pin the chest and belly piece to the body piece. Sew together with the body side up, starting at the tip and going around the entire perimeter. Trim the seams down to ⅛ in. (3 mm).

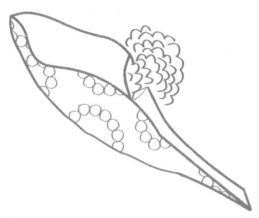

Step 5

Turn the piece right side out and gently poke out the corners. Stuff with polyester fiberfill, a small handful at a time, until it is full. Fold the raw edges of the chest and belly pieces under to match the edge seams.

Step 6

With needle and thread, do a running stitch on the chest piece that goes through both layers of the folded fabric. Gently pull the threads to gather the fabric until it matches the belly side. Knot the thread and then use the extra length to close the opening.

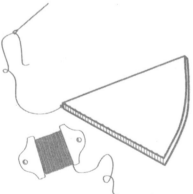

Step 7

Fold the felt in half into a cone shape. Thread the floss. Beginning at the wide opening, sew a tiny ladder stitch to sew the cone closed. Secure the floss at the end with a knot. With the needle, pull the remaining floss through the point and bring it out the open end.

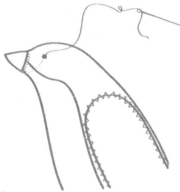

Step 8

Attach the beak to the fabric with a ladder stitch. Pull the needle through the body and bring it out where you want the eye to be. Sew the eye with satin stitch and then poke the needle through to the other side and sew the other eye.

Other ideas to try

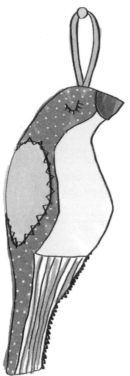

Ornament

Add a 10-in. (25.5-cm) piece of string, tiny rick rack, or ribbon into the seam of the body pieces to create an ornament. Add the string in Step 2. If you make 6 or 9 of these ornaments, they would make a sweet and original mobile for a baby's room!

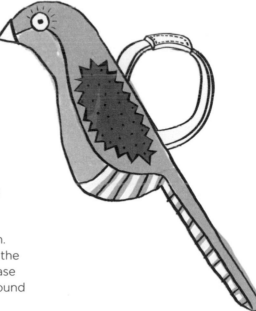

Baby toy

The Bluebird is the perfect size to make a darling baby toy. In Step 5, when stuffing the bird, add a rattle along with the stuffing and close up the bird as directed in Step 6. Create a fabric strap that will measure 1 x 7 in. (2.5 x 18 cm) when finished. Add 1-in. (2.5-cm) tabs of hook-and-loop fastener to the ends of the strap. Sew the strap onto the base of the Bluebird so that it can be secured around a baby's wrist.

Cardinal

Catching a glimpse of a bright red cardinal in the dead of Winter can make your heart skip a beat and long for Spring sunshine. Although a cardinal sighting is fairly common, the male's bright red color makes him special. Cardinals also have a lovely song that can easily be recognized if you are listening!

The peaked head and bright red of the cardinal's shape make it a wonderful sewing project. This one is reminiscent of a chubby Winter cardinal, when he is full of seed from the feeder. Try mixing lots of your red scraps together to make this bird extra bright. The felt wings are optional but give a nice texture. You could add a little cross stitch or embroidery if you want to make your bird really special.

Get stitching!

Materials needed

- Cotton scraps in shades of 1 color
- Wool felt in 2 colors
- Flannel scrap
- Sewing machine (optional), coordinating thread, scissors
- Chopstick for turning
- Polyester fiberfill
- Separated coordinating embroidery floss and needle
- 2 x ¼-in. (6-mm) buttons

Pattern measures

Height: 3 ½ in (9 cm)
Length: 5 ½ in (14 cm)

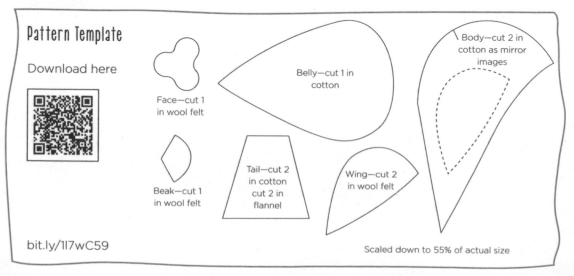

Pattern Template

Download here

bit.ly/1l7wC59

Face—cut 1 in wool felt

Belly—cut 1 in cotton

Body—cut 2 in cotton as mirror images

Beak—cut 1 in wool felt

Tail—cut 2 in cotton cut 2 in flannel

Wing—cut 2 in wool felt

Scaled down to 55% of actual size

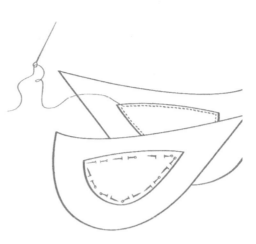

Step 1

Cut out all the pattern pieces according to the guidelines. Make sure to cut the body pieces as mirror images.

Step 2

Pin and sew wings onto the body pieces by using the placement guide on the pattern piece.

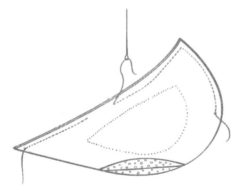

Step 3

Sew the body pieces right sides together, from the tip of the tail to the spot designated by the line on the pattern piece. Leave a 2-in. (5-cm) gap on the back for turning. Trim seams down and clip corners.

Step 4

Open up the unsewn bottom and pin the belly around the opening right sides together. It may help to mark the center of the belly piece so your Cardinal doesn't become lopsided. Sew the belly onto the body piece.

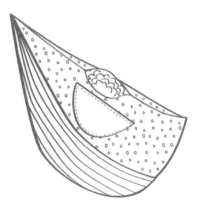

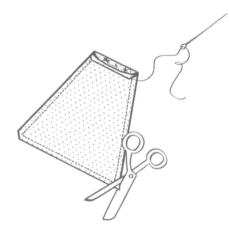

Step 5

Trim down the seams and turn the piece right side out. Poke out the pointed head with a chopstick. Stuff with polyester fiberfill and sew the opening closed with a ladder stitch or a blind stitch.

Step 6

Place flannel tail pieces behind cotton tail pieces. Pin and sew the tail pieces right sides together, leaving the short, straight end open. Trim the seams and turn the piece right side out. Poke out the corners with a chopstick. Turn the raw edges under and press flat.

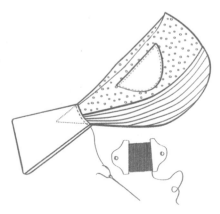

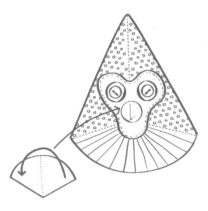

Step 7

Insert the pointed end of the body into the tail and pin. Handsew the tail onto the body with embroidery floss.

Step 8

Fold the beak in half so the straight edges line up. Sew the beak together with a ladder stitch and coordinating embroidery floss. Sew the beak centered onto the face piece. Sew the face onto the body with embroidery floss and then sew the button eyes in place.

Other ideas to try

Christmas tree ornament

Attach a loop of string or tiny rick rack to the top of the Cardinal to hang it on your Christmas tree. It would look really sweet with the new year embroidered onto the wing.

Card holder

In Step 2, when you are sewing the wings onto the body pieces, leave the top edge of one of the wings unsewn. When the piece is sewn together and stuffed, this wing becomes a pocket where you can keep business cards or other small cards.

Woodpecker

I love to hear the pecking of a woodpecker when I am on a walk or just raking leaves in the yard. Imagine a bright, colorful beauty out there, working hard! Woodpeckers are so distinctive that catching a glimpse of one always seems special.

The Woodpecker's bright, crisp colors and strong beak make it a really fun bird to sew, and it is a quick and simple project, even for beginners. I chose to make a pileated woodpecker but you can easily alter the pattern to resemble other types, such as the greater flameback, ivory-billed, or red-bellied woodpecker.

Search through your scraps to find some fun prints and top this guy off with a bright red cap. Try mixing in some different textures, such as a lightweight décor fabric and or a duck cloth or corduroy for the belly. This little Woodpecker will make a great addition to your bird collection.

Get stitching!

Materials needed

- 3 scraps of cotton fabric, 2 patterned and 1 plain
- Sewing machine (optional), coordinating thread, scissors
- Chopstick for turning
- Polyester fiberfill
- Needle and thread
- Wool felt in 2 colors
- Separated embroidery floss to coordinate with the 2 wool-felt scraps and needle
- 2 x ¼-in. (6-mm) buttons

Pattern measures

Length: 8¾ in. (22 cm)
Width: 1¾ in. (4.5 cm)

Pattern Template

Download here

bit.ly/1saat77

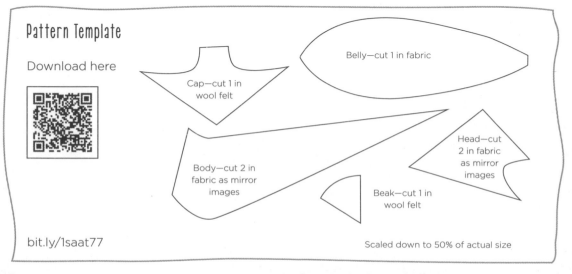

Belly—cut 1 in fabric

Cap—cut 1 in wool felt

Head—cut 2 in fabric as mirror images

Body—cut 2 in fabric as mirror images

Beak—cut 1 in wool felt

Scaled down to 50% of actual size

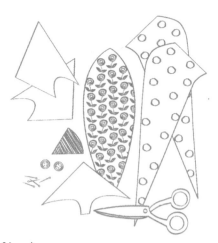 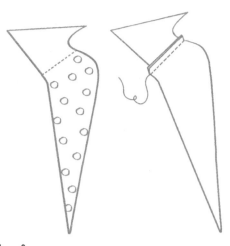

Step 1

Cut out all the pattern pieces according to the guidelines. Make sure to cut the body and head pieces as mirror images.

Step 2

With right sides together, sew the heads to the body pieces. Press the seams out flat.

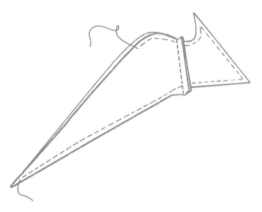 

Step 3

Pin and sew the bodies right sides together, following the line indicated on the pattern pieces, around the head and all the way down the back.

Step 4

Pin the belly to the body piece with right sides together. The curved top of the belly piece should be lined up with the seam by the head. Sew the belly and body together. leaving a 2-in. (5-cm) gap for turning.

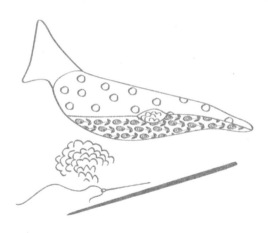

Step 5

Clip the corners and trim down the seams. Turn the piece right side out. Poke out the beak, head, and tail with a chopstick. Stuff with polyester fiberfill and sew the opening closed using ladder stitch.

Step 6

Fold the felt cap in half to make a triangle. Using the separated coordinating embroidery floss, starting at the tip, sew the cap together with a ladder stitch. Leave the long tail of the floss. Repeat with the beak, using the separated coordinating floss.

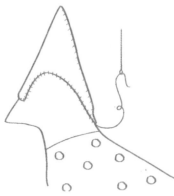

Step 7

Fit the cap snugly onto the pointed head of the bird. Using the long tail of floss from the last step, ladder stitch the cap onto the body.

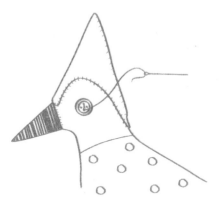

Step 8

Fit the beak onto the body. Using the tail of embroidery floss from sewing up the beak in Step 6, ladder stitch the beak to the body. Where the cap and beak meet, pull the two together gently with the floss. Sew on the button eyes.

Other ideas to try

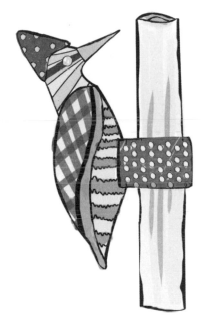

Napkin ring

Make your Woodpecker into a napkin ring by attaching it to a simple tube of fabric. Measure a piece of fabric 3 x 6 in. (7.5 x 15 cm). Fold right sides together lengthwise to create a tube. Pin and sew together but leave the short ends open. Turn right side out and press flat. Fold one raw edge under and press again. Insert the raw edge into the folded edge and pin. Handsew the loop onto the Woodpecker's belly and close up the opening at the same time. Pull a napkin through the loop and create a lovely place setting!

Fridge magnet

Glue a strong magnet to the side of the Woodpecker to create a fun magnet for the refrigerator.

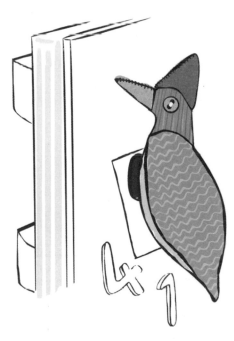

Seagull

No matter what seashore you visit, from California to Australia to France, you will most likely see seagulls. These strong and beautiful shore birds live all over the planet and, to many of us, represent a precious beach vacation. Their broad wings, crisp colors, and bright yellow beaks make them easy to recognize and admire.

This version of the seagull is cute and sturdy. It takes some balancing to make the bird stand on its wire legs, but with some practice, you can achieve a standing Seagull. Thankfully, this bird looks every bit as sweet sitting as it does standing up! Experiment with textured fabric for the belly piece, such as a lightweight cotton corduroy or linen.

Get stitching!

Materials needed

- Cotton fabric scraps in 2 colors
- Sewing machine (optional), coordinating thread, scissors
- Cotton batting or flannel scrap
- Polyester fiberfill
- 6½ in. (16.5 cm) of ¼-in (6-mm) bendable coated wire
- Separated coordinated embroidery floss and needle
- Glue
- Wool felt scraps
- 2 x ½-in. (1.3-cm) buttons

Pattern measures

Length: 8¼ in. (21 cm)
Width: 3¼ in. (9 cm)

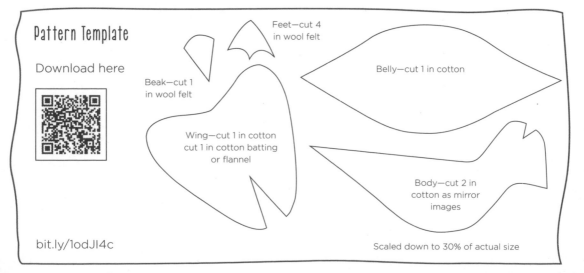

Pattern Template

Download here

Feet—cut 4 in wool felt

Beak—cut 1 in wool felt

Belly—cut 1 in cotton

Wing—cut 1 in cotton cut 1 in cotton batting or flannel

Body—cut 2 in cotton as mirror images

bit.ly/1odJI4c

Scaled down to 30% of actual size

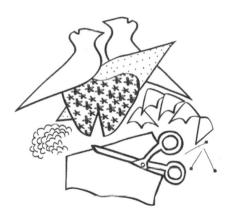

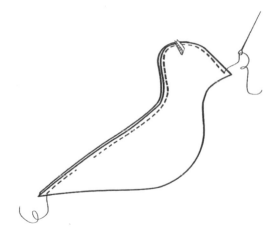

Step 1

Cut out all the pattern pieces according to the guidelines. Make sure to cut the body pieces as mirror images.

Step 2

Sew darts on the body pieces by folding the cutout triangle on the head right sides together and sewing it closed. Starting at the pointed tip, sew along the back to the point where the beak will be. Leave a 2-in. (5-cm) opening for turning.

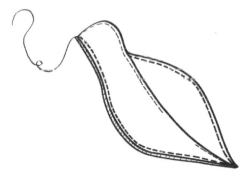

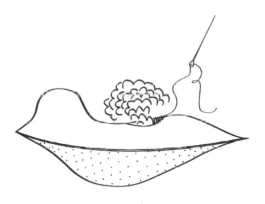

Step 3

Open up the body piece and pin right sides together to the belly piece. Sew around the entire perimeter of the belly. If you work on the body side, it is easier to get a good fit.

Step 4

Trim the seams and clip the corners. Turn right side out and stuff with polyester fiberfill. Sew the opening closed with a ladder stitch. This will be covered by the wing, so it doesn't have to be perfect.

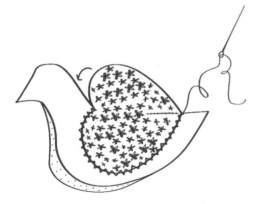

Step 5

Place the wing piece on top of the matching cotton-batting piece. Make the dart by folding the right sides together and sewing closed. Zigzag stitch around the perimeter as close to the edge as possible. Use overcast stitch if handsewing. Pin the wing to the body and handsew it on.

Step 6

Bend the wire into a U shape and flatten the center section. Bend the ends forward to make "feet." Spread glue on one side of the wire. Cut a long piece of embroidery floss. Starting at the bend of the foot, wrap the floss around the wire.

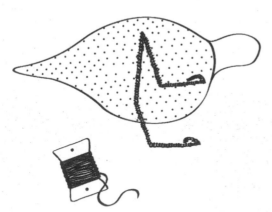

Step 7

When you get to the flat center section, use a needle to attach the floss to the body in close loops. When you get to the next bend, spread glue on the wire again and wrap the rest of the floss around the wire down to the next bend.

Step 8

Sew together the felt feet, leaving the back open. Dab glue on the wire ends and insert them into the feet. Fold the straight edges of the beak together and sew them using a ladder stitch. Attach the beak. Place felt circles under the buttons and sew them to the face.

Other ideas to try

Seagull bunting

Use the template on page 120 to cut out a flattened version of the Seagull body and wing. Use the body pattern piece and cut two from quilting-weight cotton and one from cotton batting. Cut out one wing piece (or two if you want your Seagull to be two sided). Zigzag stitch the wing in place on one of the cotton body pieces with the cotton batting layered behind it. Use overcast stitch if handsewing. Sew the cotton body pieces right sides together and leave a 2½-in. (6.5-cm) opening on the bottom. Turn the piece right side out, poke out the beak, and press flat. Blind stitch the opening closed. Make beak as directed in Step 8 and attach to body. Make a few Seagulls and handsew them onto a rope to create bunting.

Bookend

To make the Seagull into a stylish beachy bookend, increase the size to 125%. Fill the Seagull mostly with rice and then finish the head with polyester fiberfill in Step 4. Finish the Seagull as directed and place it on your bookshelf.

Chick

Chicks are particularly cute baby birds. You don't have to make your chicks yellow. Their shape is so distinctive that you can make them in a rainbow of colors and it will still be obvious they are chicks. You could add multicolored chicks to your Easter baskets and spring décor for an adorable handmade look.

Using wool felt on the base of this little Chick gives it extra sturdiness and a sweet look, but it could easily be replaced with cotton fabric or flannel. Try weighting the bottom of your Chick with rice or popcorn to make it extra sturdy. This is a quick and easy project so after you make your first one, plan on making a bunch more!

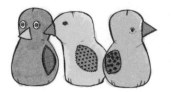

Get stitching!

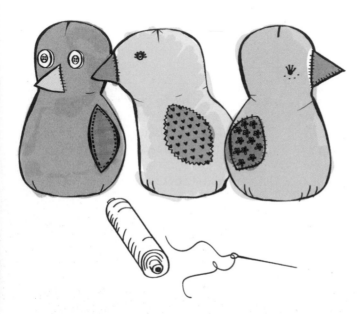

Materials needed

- Cotton fabric scraps in 2 colors
- Wool felt
- Sewing machine (optional), coordinating thread, scissors
- Separated coordinated embroidery floss and needle
- Polyester fiberfill
- 2 small buttons

Pattern measures

Height: 4½ in. (11.5 cm)
Width: 2¼ in. (6 cm)

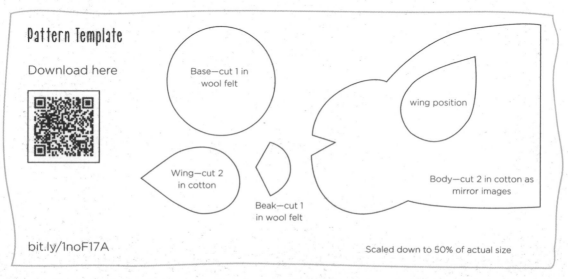

Pattern Template

Download here

Base—cut 1 in wool felt

wing position

Wing—cut 2 in cotton

Beak—cut 1 in wool felt

Body—cut 2 in cotton as mirror images

bit.ly/1noF17A

Scaled down to 50% of actual size

Step 1

Cut out all the pattern pieces according to the guidelines. Make sure to cut the body pieces in mirror images.

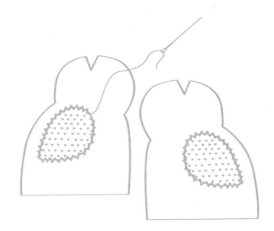

Step 2

Use the pattern pieces to guide the wing placement. Either straight stitch or zigzag stitch the wings in place on the body pieces. Use overcast stitch if handsewing.

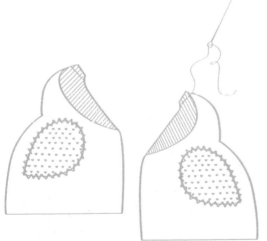

Step 3

To make the darts, fold the triangular openings at the top of the bodies right sides together and sew closed.

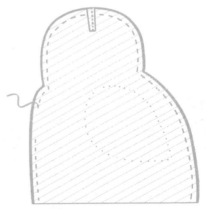

Step 4

Pin the body pieces right sides together and sew around the perimeter. Leave a 2-in. (5-cm) opening on the side for turning and leave the bottom open. Finger press the seams open and trim down the seams.

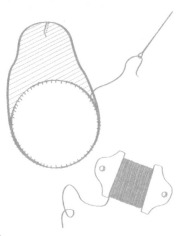

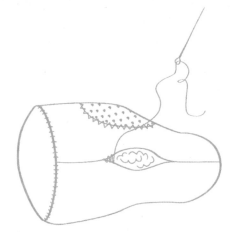

Step 5

Using separated embroidery floss, sew the wool-felt circle onto the body with a ladder stitch. Alternatively, you can sew it on with a sewing machine.

Step 6

Turn the piece right side out through the opening. Stuff it with polyester fiberfill. Close the opening with a blind stitch or a tiny ladder stitch.

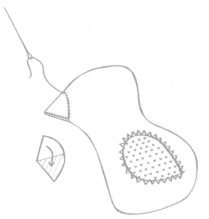

Step 7

Fold together the straight edges of the wool-felt beak. Starting at the point, ladder stitch closed with embroidery floss. Use the rest of the floss to sew the beak onto the Chick's body.

Step 8

Sew on the button eyes.

Other ideas to try

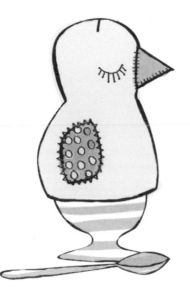

Egg cozy

Cut four body pieces, two for the lining and two for the outside. Attach wings to the two outside body pieces. In Step 3, sew the darts together on all four body pieces. In Step 4, sew together the two outside body pieces and the two lining pieces but leave a 2-in. (5-cm) opening on the lining pieces. Turn the outside body pieces right side out. Insert the outside pieces inside the lining pieces and sew the bottoms together. Pull the project right side out through the opening in the lining. Close the opening with a ladder stitch or with a sewing machine. Push the lining inside the outside. Attach the beak and eyes.

Pocket-tissue holder

When you cut out the body pieces, layer a folded piece of fabric that is half the height behind one of the fabric pieces. Cut the folded fabric along with the pattern pieces. Omit cutting the dart. Add the wing to only one side; the other side has the pocket. Sew the layers right sides together around the entire perimeter. Close the bottom edge. Leave a 2-in. (5-cm) gap on one edge.

Turn the project right side out and iron flat. Handsew the opening closed and sew a triangle beak and an eye to the side of the Chick with the wing. You can put a packet of tissues in the pocket on the other side.

Robin

Robins are beloved for their cheery disposition, bright red breast, and their appearance in early spring. Their presence after the cold winter months brings the promise of spring flowers and mild weather. Robins are strong and sturdy birds and have long been part of folklore. It is said the robin got its red breast by fanning the flames of a campfire to save the lives of a Native American boy and his father.

This scrap-fabric version resembles the American robin but can be easily altered to resemble its European cousin. This Robin features a sturdy fabric body, a bright red breast, gathered wings, a sweet felt beak, and a small button eye. It is a simple and quick project with some straightforward handsewing. Make yourself a few of these during the doldrums of winter to remind yourself that spring is just around the corner!

Get stitching!

Materials needed

- Fabric scraps in 3 colors
- Sewing machine (optional), coordinating thread, scissors
- Chopstick for turning
- Polyester fiberfill
- Needle and thread
- Separated embroidery floss to coordinate with wings and beak, and needle
- Scrap of wool felt
- 2 x ½-in. (1.3-cm) or smaller buttons

Pattern measures

Height: 4¾ in. (12 cm)
Width: 3 in. (8 cm)

Pattern Template

Download here

bit.ly/1hCpdGX

Breast—cut 1 in fabric and make center crease with fingers.

Wing—cut 4 in fabric and leave a 1½ in.- (3.8-cm) opening

Beak—cut 1 in wool felt

Body—cut 2 in fabric as mirror images

Scaled down to 40% of actual size

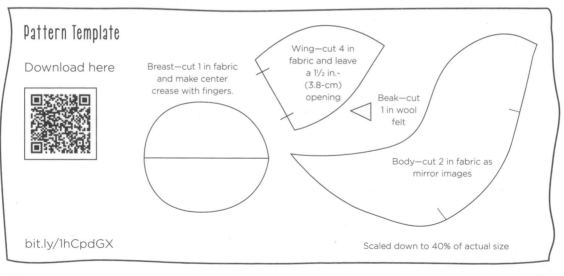

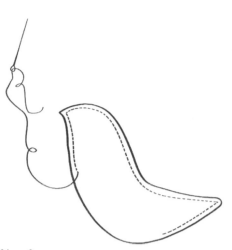

Step 1

Cut out all the pattern pieces according to the guidelines. Make sure to cut the body pieces as mirror images.

Step 2

Place the two body pieces right sides together and sew around the perimeter. Leave a gap as indicated on the pattern piece. Trim down the seams and clip the pointed ends.

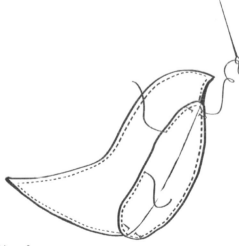

Step 3

Fold the breast piece in half lengthwise. Finger press to make a clear center line. Use this line to pin the top and base to the body pieces at the body piece seams, with right sides together. Sew the belly and body pieces together, leaving a 2-in. (5-cm) gap for turning.

Step 4

Turn the piece right side out. Poke out the tail and beak with a chopstick. Stuff with polyester fiberfill and handsew the opening closed with a ladder stitch.

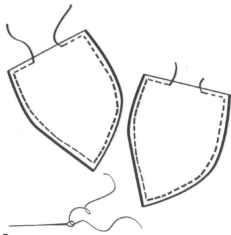

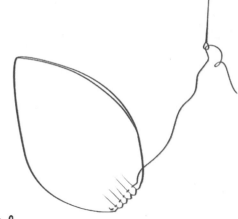

Step 5

Place the two wing-fabric pieces together with right sides facing. Sew around the perimeter of the wings, leaving a 1½-in. (4-cm) gap on the straight edge. Trim down the seams and clip the corners. Turn the wing right side out and press flat. Repeat with the other wing pieces.

Step 6

Press the wing opening under to match the seams. Tie a knot at the end of the coordinating embroidery floss and sew a small running stitch along the straight edge. Gently pull the thread to gather the fabric and tie a knot to secure it.

Step 7

Pin the wing to the body. Handsew it in place with the remaining embroidery thread. Repeat with the other wing on the other side of the body.

Step 8

Fold the felt piece in half and sew closed with a ladder stitch and the coordinating embroidery thread. Use remaining thread to attach the beak to the bird body. Sew on the button eyes.

Get stitching!

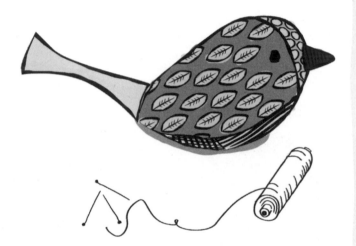

Materials needed

- Cotton fabric scraps in shades of 1 color
- Sewing machine (optional), coordinating thread, scissors
- Chopstick for turning
- Polyester fiberfill
- Needle and thread
- Scrap of wool felt
- Separated coordinated embroidery floss and needle

Pattern measures

Length: 6 in. (15 cm)
Width: 2 ¾ in. (7 cm)

Pattern Template

Download here

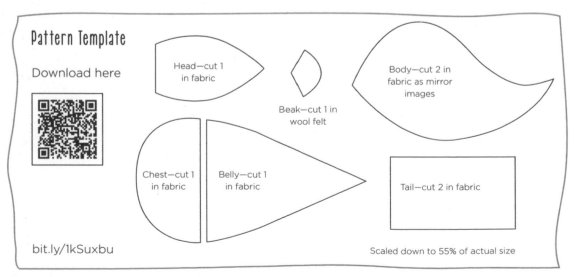

Head—cut 1 in fabric

Beak—cut 1 in wool felt

Body—cut 2 in fabric as mirror images

Chest—cut 1 in fabric

Belly—cut 1 in fabric

Tail—cut 2 in fabric

bit.ly/1kSuxbu

Scaled down to 55% of actual size

Step 1

Cut out all the pattern pieces according to the guidelines. Make sure to cut the body pieces in mirror images.

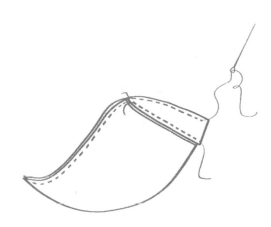

Step 2

With right sides together, sew the head piece to a body piece. With right sides together, sew the other side of the head piece to the other body piece. Sew the back of the body pieces right sides together down to the curved tip of the body.

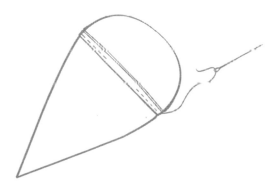

Step 3

Pin the straight edges of the belly and chest pattern pieces right sides together. Do not sew the entire way across but instead sew just ¾ in. (2 cm) in on each side and leave the center open for turning the piece right side out. Finger press the seam open.

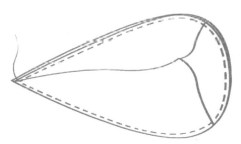

Step 4

Pin right sides together of the belly/chest piece and the head/body piece. Sew together around the perimeter. Trim down the seams.

Step 5

Pull the piece right side out through the chest/belly opening. Poke out the tail with a chopstick. Stuff full with polyester fiberfill and handsew closed with a tiny ladder stitch.

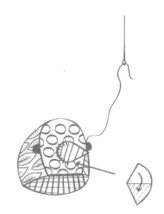

Step 6

Pin and sew the tail pieces right sides together but leave one of the short ends open for turning. Clip the corners and trim down the seams. Turn right side out and poke out the corners. Fold 1/4 in. (6 mm) of the raw edge inside and press the piece flat.

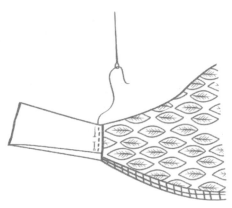

Step 7

Slide the tail over the pointed end of the body until it fits snugly. Pin to secure. Use the embroidery floss and a running stitch to secure the tail to the body.

Step 8

Fold together the straight sides of the beak. Starting at the point, sew together with the floss using ladder stitch. Use the tail of the floss to attach the beak to the flat "face" of the bird. Use the remaining floss to embroider the eyes in satin stitch.

Other ideas to try

Paperweight

Fill your Wren half with stuffing and half with rice so you can use it as a paperweight. Why not use it to weight your pattern pieces while you're working on projects?

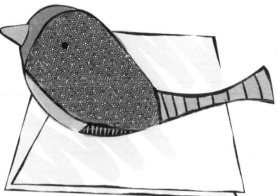

Mobile

Make several Fairy Wrens and hang them from an embroidery hoop to make a decoration for a small child's room.

Swan

It's hard to think of any birds more elegant than swans. Their long, curved necks and lovely shape are just so pretty and calming. Swans are known to mate for life, so they often represent fidelity, marriage, and loyalty. They also make a straightforward, enjoyable sewing project!

Since swans are almost all white, this is a great project for mixing textures and using some scraps of fabric with just a little bit of color. I used flannel, vintage sheets with tiny roses, and cotton chenille for the wings. If you do mix textures, use fabrics with a similar amount of stretch so the shape stays the same. With the pretty curve of the neck on the Swan, it is important to clip the curves and trim down the seam allowance before you turn the piece right side out. Do this by making 'clips' (triangular shapes with your scissors) along the curvy neck. Get close to the seam, but do not actually cut it. This will get rid of the bulky seam allowance and make the curve of your Swan's neck extra pretty.

Get stitching!

Materials needed

- Scraps of fabric in 1 color
- Sewing machine (optional), coordinating thread, scissors
- Polyester fiberfill
- Wool felt scraps in 2 colors
- Separated coordinated embroidery floss and needle
- 2 x ½-in. (1.3-cm) buttons

Pattern measures

Height: 8 in. (20 cm)
Length: 8¾ in. (22 cm)

Pattern Template

Download here

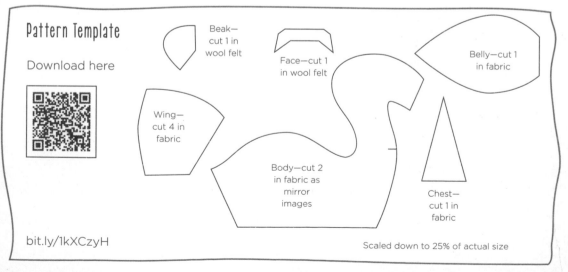

Beak—cut 1 in wool felt

Face—cut 1 in wool felt

Belly—cut 1 in fabric

Wing—cut 4 in fabric

Body—cut 2 in fabric as mirror images

Chest—cut 1 in fabric

bit.ly/1kXCzyH

Scaled down to 25% of actual size

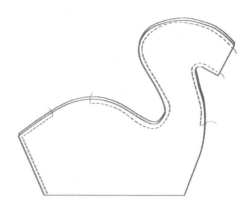

Step 1

Cut out all the pattern pieces according to the guidelines. Make sure to cut the body pieces as mirror images.

Step 2

Sew the body pieces right sides together, starting at the back edge. Leave the straight bottom edge open. Leave a 2½-in. (6.5-cm) opening on the back and an opening at the head. Stop sewing at the line marked on the pattern piece.

Step 3

Sew together the chest and belly, right sides together, and press the seam out flat.

Step 4

With right sides together, sew the chest/belly piece onto the body piece. It is easiest to start at one side of the chest and then sew to the back seam, then start at the chest tip again and sew the other side.

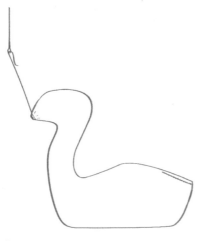

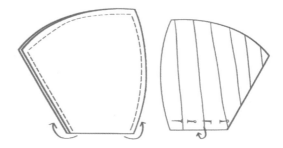

Step 5

Trim the seam and clip the corners and curves. Turn right side out and stuff with polyester fiberfill. Close the opening on the back with a ladder stitch. Sew a running stitch around the head opening and gently pull the thread to gather. Knot the thread to hold the gather.

Step 6

Sew the wings right sides together, leaving the short straight edge open. Trim the seams and corners. Turn the wing right side out and press flat. Fold raw edges under and pin closed. If you use a plain fabric, you may want to quilt a design on the wing to add interest.

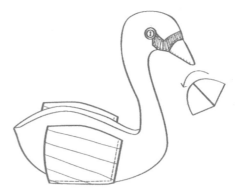

Step 7

Pin the wing to the body and sew it on with a running stitch (or ladder stitch) along the straight side toward the body front and the curved bottom edge of the wing.

Step 8

Sew the straight edges of the beak together with embroidery floss divided in half. Cover the gathered nose with the beak and sew on with a ladder stitch. Sew the felt face over the top of the beak. Sew the button eyes to the pointed edges of the face.

Other ideas to try

Peg bag

When you sew the body pieces together in
Step 2, make the opening in the back 5 in.
(12.5 cm) long. Make a pocket by folding a piece
of fabric right sides together that measures
5¼ x 7 in. (13.5 x 18 cm). Sew the sides together
and fold the raw edges over. Insert the pocket
into the opening and ladder stitch the edges
together. Finish the Swan as directed. Fill this
deep pocket with clothes pegs for a pretty and
handy helper when doing your wash!

Hand warmer

When you stuff the Swan in
Step 5, stuff the neck and top
half of the bird with polyester
fiberfill and the bottom half with
rice. Close and finish the Swan
as directed. Heat the Swan in
20-second increments in
the microwave and cradle
it between your hands on
cold evenings.

Parrot

Parrots are a large family of birds that includes about 372 species. Even though I love pretty little budgies and majestic-looking cockatoos, my favorite parrot is the scarlet macaw, with its bright rainbow of colors and long, beautiful tail feathers. Parrots are famous for more than just pretty feathers though—they are extremely clever!

To make this Parrot, choose vibrant fabrics that will contrast with each other and show off some of your favorite fabric scraps. Experiment with lengthening the tail feathers and even adding an extra "tail feather" layer of color for a more dramatic look.

Get stitching!

Materials needed

- Fabric scraps in 4 colors
- Sewing machine (optional), coordinating thread, scissors
- Pinking shears
- Polyester fiberfill
- Wool felt scraps in 3 colors
- Separated coordinating embroidery floss and needle
- 2 x ½-in. (1.3-cm) buttons

Pattern measures

Height: 10 ¼ in. (26 cm)
Width: 3½ in. (9 cm)

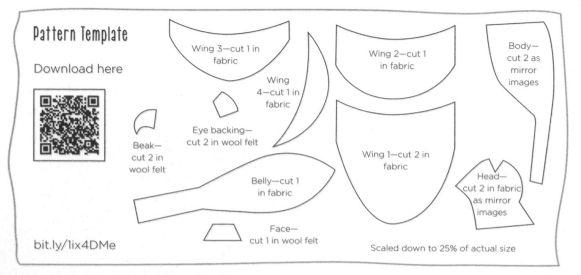

Pattern Template

Download here

bit.ly/1ix4DMe

Wing 3—cut 1 in fabric

Wing 4—cut 1 in fabric

Wing 2—cut 1 in fabric

Body—cut 2 as mirror images

Beak—cut 2 in wool felt

Eye backing—cut 2 in wool felt

Belly—cut 1 in fabric

Wing 1—cut 2 in fabric

Head—cut 2 in fabric as mirror images

Face—cut 1 in wool felt

Scaled down to 25% of actual size

Step 1

Cut out all the pattern pieces according to the guidelines. Make sure to cut the body and head pieces as mirror images.

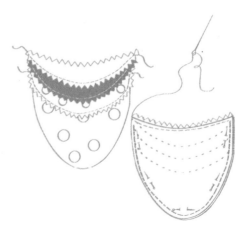

Step 2

Cut the edges of Wings 2–4 with pinking shears. Layer them right sides up on the right side of one Wing 1, according to size. Topstitch them to the wing piece. With wrong sides together, topstitch the wing layers to the other Wing 1. Finish the edges with pinking shears.

Step 3

Sew the darts on the head pieces. Sew the head pieces to the body pieces, right sides together.

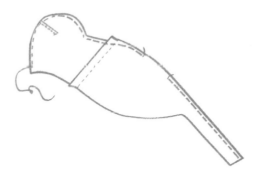

Step 4

Pin and sew the body pieces right sides together around the top of the head and down the back to the end of the tail. Leave a 2-in. (5-cm) opening on the back for turning.

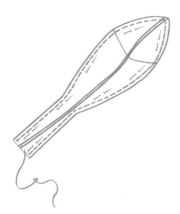

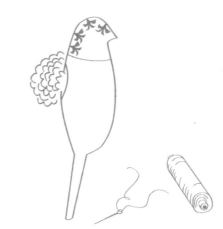

Step 5

Pin and sew the belly piece to the body pieces with right sides together.

Step 6

Trim down the seams and turn the piece right side out. Stuff full of polyester fiberfill. The stuffing will not go into the tail section and that is fine. Close the opening on the back with a ladder stitch.

Step 7

Handsew the wing over the seam that connects the head to the body. Sew the two eye backings to the face piece either with the sewing machine or by hand.

Step 8

Sew the eye backings onto the head. Put the beak pieces together and sew the curve with a ladder stitch and divided embroidery floss. Sew the sides of the beak onto the face with the remaining embroidery floss. Sew on the button eyes.

Other ideas to try

Bracelet holder

The Parrot is the perfect size for a bracelet holder. Finish the Parrot as directed and then cut a ½-in. (1.3-cm) incision in the belly. Place the Parrot on a wooden doll stand. Decorate the stand with paint or decoupage.

Travel sewing kit

Instead of sewing the wing onto the parrot at the seam of the head and body, sew the wing onto the sides at the seam where the belly and the body meet, using overcast stitch. The wing does not conform entirely to the body, so stop sewing when the wing gets too big, about three-quarters of the way down the back. Insert small scissors, a seam ripper, thread, or other sewing essentials into the pocket.

Peacock

The rich jewel-toned colors of the peacock are enough to make anyone gasp at their beauty but to see them fan their plumage is truly magnificent. In many cultures, peacocks represent vanity, owing to their extraordinary display and the way they parade around like princes. This makes them really fun to recreate with your favorite fabrics!

When selecting fabric scraps for your Peacock, go for bright tones to represent its brilliant colors. You may want to add some interfacing or an extra layer of fabric to stiffen the tail feathers so they stand up straight. Also, think about the textures of the fabrics you use—consider using corduroy, flannel, or wool. You can mix prints together to make your Peacock extra special.

Get stitching!

Materials needed

- Fabric scraps, 2 in shades of color 1 and 2 in shades of color 2, 1 solid and 1 patterned
- Sewing machine (optional), coordinating thread, scissors
- Wool felt in 3 colors
- Separated coordinating embroidery floss and needle
- Polyester fiberfill

Pattern measures

Height: 6 in. (15 cm)
Width: 9 in. (22.5 cm)

Pattern Template

Download here

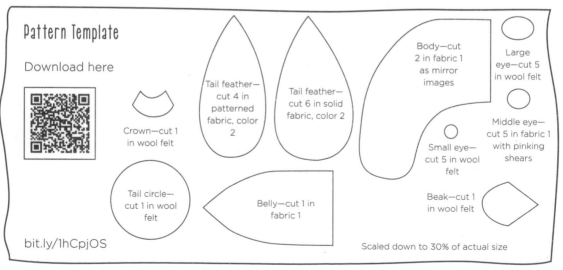

bit.ly/1hCpjOS

Crown—cut 1 in wool felt

Tail feather—cut 4 in patterned fabric, color 2

Tail feather—cut 6 in solid fabric, color 2

Body—cut 2 in fabric 1 as mirror images

Large eye—cut 5 in wool felt

Middle eye—cut 5 in fabric 1 with pinking shears

Small eye—cut 5 in wool felt

Tail circle—cut 1 in wool felt

Belly—cut 1 in fabric 1

Beak—cut 1 in wool felt

Scaled down to 30% of actual size

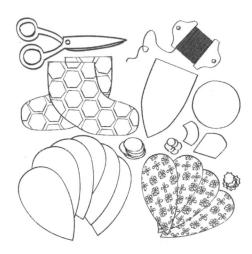

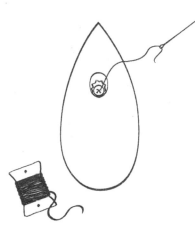

Step 1

Cut out all the pattern pieces according to the guidelines. Make sure to cut the body pieces as mirror images.

Step 2

Layer the "eyes" onto the tail feathers. First use one piece of tail fabric, then a large eye, middle eye, and small eye. With coordinating embroidery floss, sew together the four layers using cross stitch.

Step 3

Sew tail feathers right sides together, sandwiching the eyes and leaving a 2-in. (5-cm) opening on one side. Turn the feather inside out. Press flat and repeat to make five tail feathers. Close the openings with a blind stitch. Layer the feathers in the shape of a fan and pin them together.

Step 4

Center the felt circle in the middle of the tail feathers. Sew the circle onto the feathers with three circles, each getting smaller toward the center of the circle.

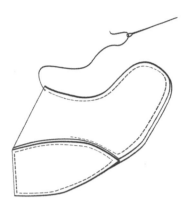

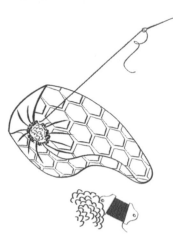

Step 5

Sew body pieces right sides together but leave the straight edge open. Sew the belly piece, right sides together, onto either side of the body pieces.

Step 6

Trim the seams and turn the body right side out. Fill with polyester fiberfill. Knot one end of embroidery floss, and sew a running stitch around the entire opening about ¼ in. (6 mm) from the raw edge. Gently pull the thread to gather the opening closed. Knot to secure.

Step 7

With coordinating floss and a ladder stitch, sew the body onto the tail feathers, centering it on the lower half of the circle so that a crescent of the tail-feather felt circle is showing above the body. Attach the feet to the bottom of the body with the remaining floss.

Step 8

Fold the straight edges of the felt beak together and, starting at the tip, sew the beak together with a ladder stitch. Attach the beak and the crown to the head with a ladder stitch. Either embroider eyes onto the head or sew on tiny buttons.

Other ideas to try

Barrette holder

Attach a loop of floss to the top of the Peacock's center tail feather. Attach a piece of ribbon 18 in. (45.5 cm) long by 1 in. (2.5 cm) wide to the back so that it hangs down. Hang the Peacock on the wall in the bathroom or bedroom and use as a barrette holder.

Letter holder

Make the tail feathers stiffer by adding a layer of interfacing (fusible or non-fusible) inside each of the five tail-feather pieces. When stuffing the body of the Peacock in Step 6, stuff the neck with polyester fiberfill and the rest with rice to make it heavier. Finish the rest of the steps as directed.

Cut a piece of cardboard 8.5 by 6 in. (21.5 x 15 cm). Cover it by making a sleeve of fabric or felt. Attach the sturdy Peacock to the covered cardboard at the base only, and place on your desk.

Hummingbird

Even if you see them regularly, the sighting of hummingbirds is always special. Their beautiful bright colors, tiny size, and super-fast movements make them unique among birds. Seeing a hummingbird is like glimpsing a little bit of magic!

The vibrant colors of this Hummingbird make it perfect to sew with your scrap fabrics. When searching for the right materials to use, consider the beautiful jewel tones of real hummingbirds. There are more than 300 types of hummingbirds so there are a huge number of possibilities. Their colors are amazing, and you can try to recreate them with your fabrics. This project is a little more detailed than some of my other birds, but the result is very special and worth the extra effort.

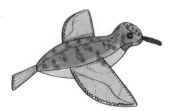

Get stitching!

Materials needed

- Fabric scraps in 3 colors
- Fusible interfacing
- Sewing machine (optional), thread, scissors
- Polyester fiberfill
- Needle and thread
- 2-in. (5-cm) piece of ¼-in. (6-mm)-thick wire
- Separated brown embroidery floss
- 2 x ¼-in. (6-mm) buttons

Pattern measures

Length: 6½ in. (17 cm)
Width: 7½ in. (19 cm)

Pattern Template

Download here

bit.ly/1jp4Z8m

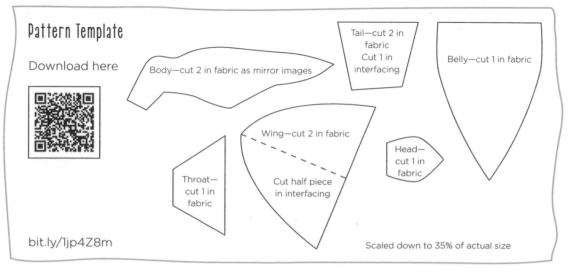

Body—cut 2 in fabric as mirror images

Tail—cut 2 in fabric
Cut 1 in interfacing

Belly—cut 1 in fabric

Wing—cut 2 in fabric

Cut half piece in interfacing

Head—cut 1 in fabric

Throat—cut 1 in fabric

Scaled down to 35% of actual size

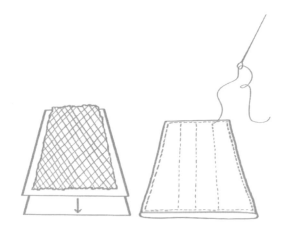

Step 1

Cut out all the pattern pieces according to the guidelines. Make sure the body pieces are cut as mirror images.

Step 2

Fuse interfacing to the wrong sides of the wing and tail pieces. Sew right sides of the tail together, leaving an opening for turning. Trim seams, turn right side out, and press flat. Topstitch around the perimeter and topstitch vertical lines for reinforcement.

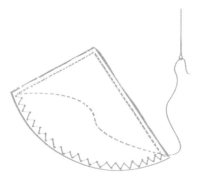

Step 3

Fold a wing piece right sides together. Sew the short straight sides together. Trim the seams and turn right side out. Press flat. Zigzag stitch along the curved edge or use overcast stitch if handsewing. Topstitch over the two straight edges. Topstitch a curve through the center of the wing piece. Repeat for the other wing.

Step 4

Attach the two body pieces to either side of the head piece. Go slowly with the sewing machine or handsew the pieces together. Fold the body piece right sides together and sew from the head seam down to the end of the tail. Trim seams down and finger press the seams open.

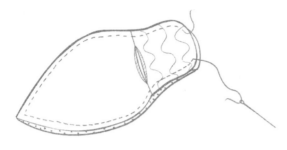

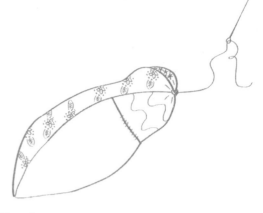

Step 5

Place belly and throat pieces right sides together. Sew ³/₄ in. (2 cm) in from either side, leaving an opening in the center. Press the seams out. Place belly/throat piece right sides together with the head/body piece. From the head, sew ³/₄ in. (2 cm) in from either side. leaving an opening in the center. Trim down the seams and clip the tail. and clip tail.

Step 6

Turn the body right side out through the throat opening. Stuff with polyester fiberfill and close with ladder stitch. Sew running stitch around the head opening. Gently pull the thread and gather the fabric closed. Knot the thread to secure the gathering.

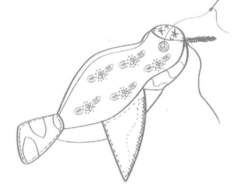

Step 7

Sew the wings and tail onto the body with ladder stitch. Place the wings along the belly and back seam, just below where the belly and throat come together. Attach the tail about an inch (2.5 cm) above the body tip.

Step 8

Push the piece of wire inside the gathered fabric you made in Step 6. Smear a little glue onto the wire and then wrap embroidery floss around wire and around the raw edge of gathered fabric area. Tie off embroidery floss. Sew on the button eyes.

Other ideas to try

Mobile

Attach clear fishing line to your Hummingbird and hang it by the window for a taste of summer year round. It will be interesting to see what real hummingbirds (who are famously territorial) think of this handmade one!

Key holder

Attach a tab to the back of your bird and he will make a striking key holder. Do this by either handsewing on a fabric loop at the end or adding a loop during Step 4. Attach a key ring to the loop and then attach to your keys.

Flamingo

Flamingos are hilarious, fascinating, and totally unique. What could be better than a bright pink bird on long, goofy legs? All teasing aside, those legs are useful for wading in the harsh wetland environment, where these extraordinary birds live. Their beautiful colors make them a really enjoyable sewing project.

Since I have three daughters, I have a big stash of pink fabric scraps. I had so much fun searching for pinks to create this Flamingo! I would suggest going for something solid or lightly printed for the body and saving your bold prints for the wing and belly. You don't want to distract from the interesting facial features. You can also adapt the length of the Flamingo's legs and make them shorter or longer if you like.

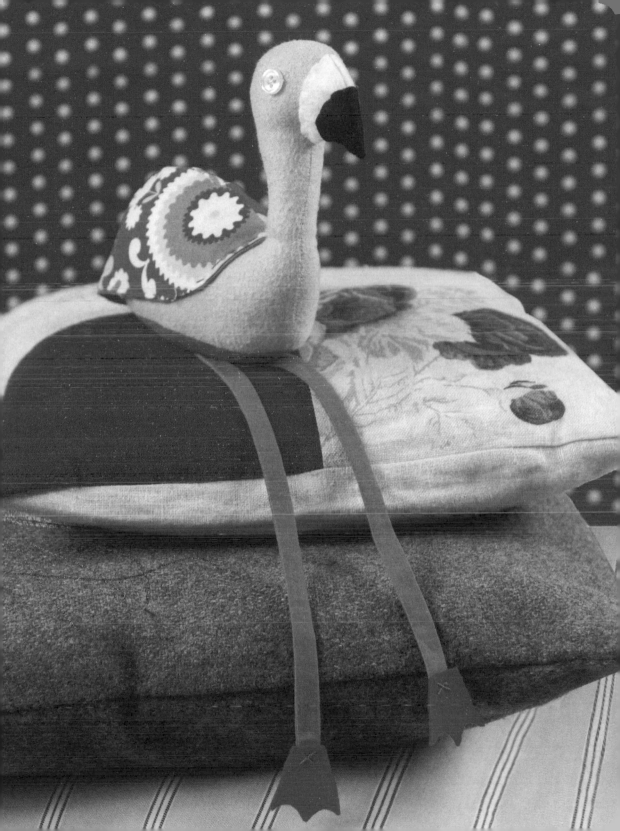

Get stitching!

Materials needed

- Fabric scraps in 4 shades of 1 color
- Sewing machine (optional), coordinating thread, scissors
- Tube turner
- Polyester fiberfill
- Wool felt scraps in 3 colors
- Separated coordinating embroidery floss and needle
- 2 x ¼-in. (6-mm) buttons

Pattern measures

Height: 16 in. (40 cm)
Width: 5½ in. (14 cm)

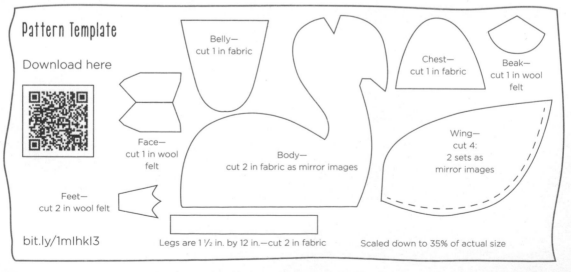

Pattern Template

Download here

bit.ly/1mlhkl3

Belly—
cut 1 in fabric

Chest—
cut 1 in fabric

Beak—
cut 1 in wool felt

Face—
cut 1 in wool felt

Body—
cut 2 in fabric as mirror images

Wing—
cut 4:
2 sets as
mirror images

Feet—
cut 2 in wool felt

Legs are 1 ½ in. by 12 in.—cut 2 in fabric

Scaled down to 35% of actual size

Step 1

Cut out all the pattern pieces according to the guidelines. Make sure to cut the body pieces as mirror images. The wing sets should also be cut as mirror images. One wing set will be the exterior and the other set will form the lining.

Step 2

Sew the darts on the heads of the body pieces and then sew the bodies, right sides together. Leave the straight bottom open.

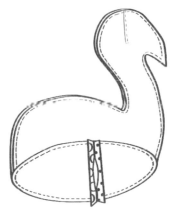

Step 3

Sew the right sides together of the belly and chest pieces at the edges only, and leave a 2-in. (5-cm) opening in the center. Sew the belly onto the body with right sides together. Trim down seams and clip corners.

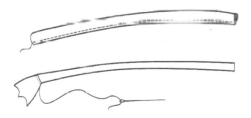

Step 4

Pin the leg pieces right sides together widthwise and sew. Trim the seams and use a tube turner to turn the legs inside out. Press flat and turn one open edge under. Press again. Sew feet to this folded-under edge with a cross stitch.

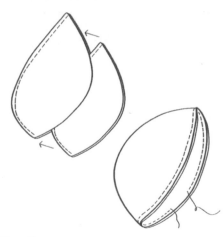

Step 5

Turn the body right side out and stuff with polyester fiberfill. Before closing the belly opening, insert the legs into the gap and use a ladder stitch to close the opening. Sew through the legs to make your stitches go through all the layers.

Step 6

Sew the two exterior wing pieces right sides together on the curve indicated on the pattern piece. Repeat with the lining set and turn the lining inside out. Insert the lining inside exterior. Pin and sew around the perimeter. Leave a 2-in. (5-cm) opening for turning. Turn, press, and close opening with a blind stitch.

Step 7

Fit the wing onto the back of the Flamingo body and sew on. Fold the face piece in half by using the line indicated. Sew the angled sides with a 1/8-in. (3-mm) seam allowance. Turn inside out and handsew onto the face using a ladder stitch.

Step 8

Fold beak in half and sew straight sides together with separated embroidery floss and a ladder stitch. Fit the beak over the felt face and sew on with a ladder stitch. Sew button eyes into place on the sides of the face.

Other ideas to try

Draft excluder

Adjust the pattern pieces to be printed at 135%. Make the Flamingo body as instructed but change the length and width of the legs to 2½ x 18 in. (6.5 x 45.5 cm). Sew the legs right sides together to make a long tube. Attach the feet as instructed in Step 4. Using a funnel, fill the legs seven-eighths full with rice. Attach legs to the body as instructed in Step 5. These long legs make a unique draft excluder.

Flamingo pillow

Print the pattern pieces at 200%. Increase the leg size to 2 x 18 in. (5 x 45.5 cm). Finish the Flamingo according to the directions. This enlarged Flamingo makes a really cute pillow for a child's bedroom.

Additional Templates

Seagull bunting

For full instructions see page 71.

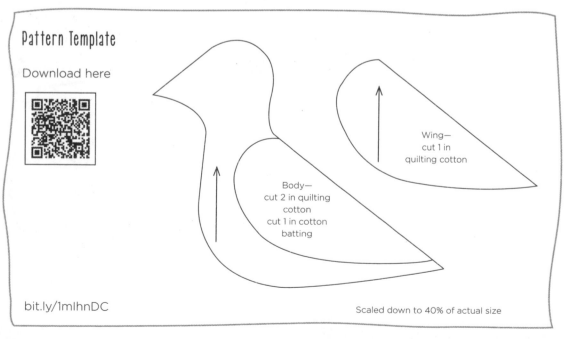

Pattern Template

Download here

bit.ly/1mlhnDC

Body—
cut 2 in quilting
cotton
cut 1 in cotton
batting

Wing—
cut 1 in
quilting cotton

Scaled down to 40% of actual size

Owl: small hot-water bottle cover

This fits a 6 x 6½ in. (15 x 16.5 cm) hot-water bottle. Use the templates on page 14 and cut out materials as on page 15. Make the Owl belly and eyes as in Step 2. Make a flap by sewing on half a piece of 1 x 5 in. (2.5 x 12.5 cm) hook-and-loop fastener to the pattern piece, folding the flap right sides together and sewing the sides. Turn the flap right side out and press flat. Attach the flap to the exterior of the Owl body according to the pattern. Layer the batting behind the lining front body piece and sew the front exterior and front lining pieces right sides together. Leave a 2½-in. (6.5-cm) opening on the side. Turn right side out and press flat. Blind stitch the opening closed. Fold down the tip and handsew it down to create the beak. Attach the eyes.

Sew the other half of the hook-and-loop fastener on the exterior back body piece according to the pattern. Layer the batting behind the lining back body piece. Sew the exterior back body and the lining back body right sides together. Leave a 2½-in. (6.5-cm) opening. Turn the piece right side out and press flat. Blind stitch the opening closed. Sandwich the front and back sides together and sew the side edges only. Insert the hot water bottle through the base and use the flap to close it.

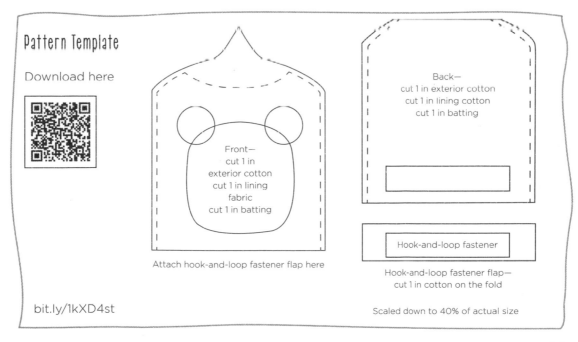

Pattern Template

Download here

Front—
cut 1 in
exterior cotton
cut 1 in lining
fabric
cut 1 in batting

Back—
cut 1 in exterior cotton
cut 1 in lining cotton
cut 1 in batting

Hook-and-loop fastener

Attach hook-and-loop fastener flap here

Hook-and-loop fastener flap—
cut 1 in cotton on the fold

bit.ly/1kXD4st

Scaled down to 40% of actual size

Glossary

backstitch When you begin to sew forward, take one stitch backward and then sew forward again. This prevents the thread from unraveling as you sew.

basting Sewing a long, loose running stitch by hand to temporarily hold fabrics together.

blanket stitch A decorative L-shaped handsewing stitch, made by looping the needle under the thread at the edge of the fabric; it reinforces the edges of the fabric.

blind stitch Handsewing technique to hide an open seam by sewing between the folds.

chain stitch Embroidery technique in which a series of loops forms a chain.

cotton batting A thick, soft layer of fabric that is usually used as the middle layer of a quilt.

cotton chenille Woven fabric with tufted velvet lines that look like long caterpillars.

dart A V-shaped, tapered adjustment that is made by sewing the angled right sides together. It adds more fullness to your piece.

decoupage Decorating an object with colored paper cutouts.

embroidery A classic handsewing technique using colored thick thread and special stitching techniques.

embroidery floss Usually six strands of colored thread, used in embroidery. In this book, we separate it into three strands. Embroidery floss can be easily found in craft stores.

fiberfill A synthetic shredded material that is used as fill in sewing projects to give three-dimensional quality.

finger press A method of temporarily flattening a seam by using the pressure and heat of your fingers.

flannel A soft cotton fabric made with a slight nap (short, fine threads lying in the same direction).

gathering A method of sewing a loose running stitch and then gently pulling the threads to bring the fabric together.

interfacing A material available in a variety of weights, thicknesses, and flexibility, used as a backing for fabrics to give them more stability. Can be fusible or sewn in.

ladder stitch Used to join two folded edges of fabric. Stitches are made at right angles to the fabric, creating a ladder-like formation between the fabrics, which is tightened and rendered less visible.

mirror image The image you would see in the mirror. Several patterns ask you to cut pattern pieces as mirror images of each other.

on the fold A term used in cutting out pattern pieces that means folding fabric in half, usually with the grain, and lining up the side designated on your pattern piece with the fold of the fabric. The fabric is cut on all sides of the pattern piece except on the fold.

overcast stitch A diagonal handstitch that loops over the fabric edge and is used to stop raw edges from fraying.

pinking shears Scissors with a V shape along the cutting edge, used to cut fabric to prevent the edges from unraveling.

raw edges Unfinished, cut edge of fabric.

rick rack A zigzag type of trim that is used to decorate and embellish items.

right side The "front" of a piece of fabric that has a distinct front and back.

running stitch The most common and basic handsewing stitch, which weaves in and out of the fabric, resulting in the look of a dashed line.

satin stitch Long, straight stitches made with embroidery floss, placed closely in rows together to give the appearance of satin.

seam allowance The area between the edge of the fabric and the stitching line on two (or more) pieces of material being stitched together.

split stitch Decorative but strong stitch made by starting with a running stitch but looping back to come up through the first stitch. The finished stitch looks like a chain.

straight stitch Stitches made with a sewing machine that create a straight line. It is the basic and most common machine stitch.

topstitch A sometimes decorative, sometimes functional stitch that is usually 1/4 in. (6 mm) from the edge of a seam and is meant to be seen on the top of the piece.

tube turner Found in the notions section at the fabric store, a long, thin plastic piece with a clip on the end that will help you to turn a long tube of fabric inside out.

wool felt A soft felt made from wool instead of synthetics, available at some crafts stores and readily available online.

wrong side The "back" of a piece of fabric that has a distinct front and back.

zigzag stitch A stitch that goes one way and then the other to provide a secure finish to a seam. It is also decorative.

Index

Acknowledgments

Thank you so much to my husband, Travis, and my children, Elsie, Anne, Calvin, and Marion for your patience, honesty, and "oohhs and ahhs" while I was creating these birds.

Thank you to my project manager and editor, Cath Senker, for your kindness, patience, and excellent skills in making my instructions simple and understandable.

Thank you to the Rotovision Editorial Director, Isheeta Mustafi, for your vision and encouragement in creating this book. Thank you to Tamsin Richardson, Assistant Editor, for your support and management skills and to Esther Richardson for helping to make some of the birds.

Thank you also to Jacqueline Ford for initially contacting me and for helping to guide this book into reality.

Thank you to my dad, Barney, for your love of birds and the many years of happiness watching the birdfeeder on the back porch. This created a fondness of birds that made creating these birds so much fun. Thank you also to my mom, Linda, for always helping me to work through ideas and your honest feedback.

Virginia Lindsay